Teenagers: The Parents'
One Hour Survival Guide

Teenagers: The Parents' One Hour Survival Guide

PAUL FRANCIS

Marshall Pickering
An Imprint of HarperCollins*Publishers*

Marshall Pickering is an imprint of HarperCollins*Religious*
Part of HarperCollins*Publishers*
77–85 Fulham Palace Road, London W6 8JB
First published in Great Britain in 1998 by Marshall Pickering

1 3 5 7 9 10 8 6 4 2
Copyright © 1998 Paul Francis

Paul Francis asserts the moral right to be identified
as the author of this work

A catalogue record for this book is available
from the British Library

ISBN 0 551 03143 3

Printed and bound in Great Britain by
Caledonian International Book Manufacturing Ltd, Glasgow

To my parents – thank you

Contents

Acknowledgements

As usual there are many people who have helped me through the task of finishing this book.

There are those who had the task of reading through early drafts: Caroline Adams, Jonathan Booth, Pat Brooks, Jacqui Butler and Rob Parsons.

Thanks must go to my colleagues and friends in work, Mark Stavers and Sharon Chapman, who never moaned (not often, anyway!) about the amount of time this work has kept me out of the office.

Special thanks to my editors, Kate Davies and James Catford.

Finally, I would like to thank Jane, who tries to live out all that we talk about.

Here and now I publicly say a heartfelt thank you to all of them. And if you enjoy and are helped by this book, you owe these people your thanks, too.

Are they from Mars?

It was an unusual party that I went to last month. The party was thrown by a good friend of mine to celebrate his son passing his exams. It was unusual in that half the guests were friends of the parents and the other half were friends of the son. Early in the evening I was in the kitchen talking to Peter, a father of a couple of young children. As we discussed football, rugby and other issues, about 30 of the son's friends arrived and walked straight into the kitchen. The conversation with Peter stopped in mid-flow and I will never forget the look on his face as they came in ... it turned from amusement, to incredulity, to fear. For as these 30 teenagers marched in they did seem very intimidating. One felt pressurized into a corner, and there was a sense of no escape! They all carried drinks, all wore the latest fashions and looked incredibly confident. This is the world of young people. It does seem such an alien world to those who've never experienced it.

It's no wonder that I'm often asked the question, 'Why are young people so different?' It's a legitimate question to ask because that really is how many people feel about young people – they seem so different, almost as if they have come from another planet. Their fashions, hair-styles, musical tastes and life ambitions all seem so alien to us that we feel they may as well have come from Mars. Well, the answer is simple – they are *not* any different! Scratch the surface and today's young people have the same (if not more) insecurities that you and I had. They wake up and look in the mirror and think, 'Why me? Why was I made to look like this? Nobody will like me – my legs are too short and my nose is too big.' Some feel they are failures while others think the world owes them a favour. In other words, they are the same as you and me!

What we do need to realize, however, is that although they may be no different to you and me, the world they live in is very different from the world we grew up in. The world of the '90s is radically changed from that of the '60s and '70s. It's their world that is alien to us, because it is far removed from anything we know.

Part of the purpose of this book is to help you understand the world your children are living in. If we can begin to understand it then we can learn from it, and can also find ways of guiding our children through all the dangers that could be waiting for them.

Perhaps some of you, as parents, are struggling with your daughter. She seems out of control, in what she wears, who she goes out with and where she goes. You are worried about how, when and what to talk to her about sex. Some of you, perhaps, are worried that your son is being pressurized by his 'friends' to take drugs. You don't know where or who to turn to. Perhaps some of you, as parents, have given up the battle because it all just seems too hard. Or perhaps some of you are just starting out.

We can't stand with our kids as they queue to go into the club where they may be offered drugs. We can't stand with our kids as their mates try to pressurize them into doing things they really do not want to do. But we can build frameworks into their lives that will help them make right decisions. That is the purpose of this book. I hope you will stick with it, and that it will begin to give you some hope. Dip in and find what helps you. I have presented 11 goals which I believe can help make a start. I don't promise any easy answers because there are none, but I hope that together we can begin to do something about the problem.

To encourage you let me finish with a quote:

> Youth has not regard for old age, and the wisdom of centuries is looked down upon both as stupidity and foolishness. The young men are indolent; the young women are indecent and indecorous in their speech, behaviour and dress.[1]

That was written by a man in 1114. Some things never change!

I want to be loved and accepted totally apart from what I do. The fear of having to perform to be accepted dominates the thought life of most teenagers. All of us are driven to be accepted and loved. When we discover an unconditional love and acceptance from our parents, we are set free from trying to earn a dominating, emotionally draining performance-based love.[2]

To understand the world of young people

As we saw in the introduction, the world in which young people are growing up has changed. It is this change that is frightening. To help you understand what is going on I have highlighted four areas where major changes have taken place.

1. Their world

When I visit schools, I often stand in front of 300 14-year-old pupils (Year 10) and ask a simple question; 'How many of you know for sure somebody who is taking a drug, excluding alcohol and tobacco?' Two-thirds of the hands go up. We need to understand that while not every young person is taking a 'recreational' drug, if a young person chooses to it is a socially accepted 'norm'. In the '60s and '70s drug taking was not the socially accepted norm. Today the climate has changed: if you want to take drugs it is considered acceptable in the world of young people.

Take the same number of Year 10 pupils: according to all the current research about 180 of them will have had sexual intercourse. (Now please note this also means that

120 have not.) What this means is that if you choose to have sex with your partner, it is an accepted norm. Again, in the '60s and '70s young people were having sex, but it was not the socially accepted norm. Today, if you want to have sex with your partner, it is considered acceptable in the world of young people.

Recently the BBC screened a new film starring Dawn French, *Chocolate and Sex*. It was a gentle, amusing story of a marriage that was working well. However, Bev Bodger, the character played by Dawn French is persuaded to visit Paris with an old school friend who has only one thing on his mind – having sex with her. She refuses and goes back home to her husband who, on discovering where she has been, throws her out of the house. The film finishes with a moving scene where the husband and wife decide to give their marriage another go. It is a simple story pretending to be nothing else.

The critics blasted it: 'too sugary', said one; 'get real', was another comment. But the most disturbing comment came from a leading newspaper columnist who said she thought it was awful because nobody comes from such a happy family anymore. And she went on to point out that no woman in Britain today has only ever had sex with only one person.

This is the world of young people – no chance of a happy family life and no chance of sticking with one partner for life.

2. Their values

A. TRUTH

A friend of mine teaches religious education in a large comprehensive school. Recently, he had the difficult task of teaching the ten commandments and to try to 'spice' it up he devised a clever questionnaire. He asked the young people to list those commandments that they thought were still relevant and those that they thought were of no relevance to today's world. The answers were 'interesting', to say the least. 'Do not kill' was still considered to be very appropriate. But the commandment which they all thought was out of date was 'Do not lie'. Only 20% of the class thought telling the truth had any relevance to today's world.

Distorting the truth is considered to be acceptable in this world. It is the perceived 'norm' for politicians and those in power. Our very fabric of society is now built on mistrust, so we have great difficulty in knowing who is right and who is wrong.

On a more positive note, once young people grasp an issue of 'truth' they will fight for it. For example, they have a great passion for the environment and for animal rights. They value the planet they live on and do not want to see it exploited. This is best illustrated by 'Swampy' and his friends. They were a group of mostly young people who felt passionately about the building of roads and extensions to airports in designated 'green' areas. They felt so strongly about the issue that they organized protests and tapped into a ground-swell of support. Young people have a concern for animals – sometimes it's misplaced and sometimes it goes to extremes – but there is still a concern and care.

B. LIVE FOR THE MOMENT
One only needs to spend a short time watching some of the 'youth orientated' television programmes to discover the speed of things. *Big Breakfast* and *TFI Friday* are as good models as you will find. They are very fast moving, never

giving much time to any one sequence. They are full of a lot of amusing trivia and well hosted. After you have watched them you may have had fun but did you come away with any substantial information? No! They say everything about our modern culture.

The programmes are designed on the assumption that most young people have a short concentration span, and if you don't keep engaging it they will move on to something else. So to stop that the programme keeps changing. The content is often a mixture of the bizarre and the informative – but never so much that they lose people's attention.

It is also reflected by the band the Spice Girls, not so much by their lyrics but by their whole attitude. It's an attitude that simply says: live for the moment, enjoy today and don't worry about tomorrow.

They are representative of our modern culture; young people are like that. They move from one experience to another for no other reason than they have got bored with the previous experience. It is reflected in the drug culture where they may try ecstasy, then cannabis, then speed and so on, the only reason being that they want new and different experiences.

3. Their fears

There is a joke that is currently going round the university campuses:

Q: What do you say to a graduate with a job?
A: Big Mac and fries, please.

Now in no way is that meant to be an insult to those who work in burger bars, but you don't need a degree to work there. The joke, rather, is a reflection of the fact that nothing is guaranteed any more. In the '60s and '70s, you went to university, got a degree and almost walked straight into a job. Today's young people can get to university but there is little guarantee of a job. They also have the 'small' problem of the student loan system with the average student leaving college with an £8,000 loan to pay off. Is it any wonder that anxiety is high on their list of used words?

I originate from the north-east of England and on return trips my father will often point out where there used to be collieries; now all you see is a lake, or a hill or ploughed fields. But for many years the coal industry was a major supplier of work. Generation would follow generation down the mines. Now there is no such option: the mines have long closed and a job for life is a dream of a bygone era.

Back in the '60s and '70s science was seen as the god that could save us from all ills. Oil and gas were available in unlimited supplies and the future was there for the taking. Now science seems to have created as many problems as it seems to answer. We are on the brink of an environmental disaster. There are emission gases that are affecting the ozone layer, there are pesticides that are polluting our land and there is erosion of vast areas of land.

In short, young people look to the future and see little hope. It's reflected in the music of bands such as Nirvana, the Manic Street Preachers, the Verve and so on. They have little hope in politics as they constantly feel let down by politicians. They despair for the environment and the way in which we are raping the world. Two words sum up the fears of young people: no hope.

The result is that we have created a young generation that no longer trusts or believes in anything. It's a generation that is suspicious of those in power and believes there are hidden agendas behind everything. It is a generation with a disturbingly high rate of suicides and eating disorders. Basically, it is a generation that is very insecure.

4. Hope

Much of modern Britain is dark, a reality that is reflected in much of our culture. Irvine Welsh's portrait of life in *Trainspotting* is brilliant but bleak; *The Full Monty* and *Brassed Off* are powerful films but portray communities that are breaking up. The artist Damien Hirst's work is full of images about death. The whole generation was captured by Johnny Davis in an interview in *The Face* magazine.

> ... an audience weathered by drugs and insecurities, an audience for whom lyrics of pain, trouble and loss, of admitting your shortcomings, make great sense.

In short, the young do not have much hope and simply want to live for the moment. So we may well ask, '**is there any hope?**'

Hang on in there because I believe that there *is* hope. I have a great belief that young people do listen to advice if it is given in the right way. I have a great belief that if they are given *all* the information they will make informed choices. As we go through this one-hour guide, I hope that together we can learn ways to begin to tackle these big issues. I believe there is hope because I constantly meet young people who want to live a better way. So read on ... there is always hope!

These quotes from contemporary sources aptly describe the world of young people.

I think I know a person then, poof! I discover I only knew a cartoon version ... unknowable and just as lost as I am, and equally unable to remember that every soul in the world is hurting, not just themselves.
Douglas Coupland, *Shampoo Planet*[3]

It's all just a random lottery of meaningless tragedy and a series of near escapes. So I take pleasure in the details, like a quarter-pounder with cheese.
From the film *Reality Bites*

I mean, how can you be a spokesman for a generation if you've nothing to say other than HELP.
Bono, *U2*

I had thought I was finding consolation in solitude, but to be honest, I think I was only acquiring a veneer of bitter-ness ... loneliness had of late become an emotion I had stopped feeling so intensely ... But I realised the capacity for not feeling lonely carried a very real price, which was the threat of feeling nothing at all.
Douglas Coupland, *Life after God*[4]

STATS THAT SAY A LOT

At any one time in the UK about 60,000 people may be psychiatrically ill with the eating disorders anorexia nervosa or bulimia nervosa.[5]

Twenty years ago models weighed 8% less than the average woman: now they weigh 23% less.[6]

In a recent US survey 11% of parents said they would abort a child predisposed to obesity [7]

The suicide rate amongst UK males aged between 13 and 24 rose by 71% between 1982 and 1992. [8]

LINES THAT LAST

Amy, 16, 'Everywhere I look there are skinny people, which makes me hate myself even more. I wish magazines would stop portraying "fat" as being bad.'

Jacqueline, 17, 'I try to like myself for what I am but I open a magazine and immediately compare myself with those perfect models.'[9]

To understand the forces shaping your children's world

Her hair is long and gently flows in the air as she runs towards you. Her dress is beautifully fitted and her make-up is perfect. The day is glorious with a strange haze that hangs in the air. You stand by the car, wearing your black Armani suit, green shirt and brogue shoes. Your chisel-like chin is slightly lifted and a smile flickers across your face. As your eyes meet the smile breaks into laughter and two sets of perfect white teeth greet each other. From somewhere an orchestra plays and in your heart – this is heaven – the girl of your dreams is in your arms. Somewhere a voice shouts 'Cut!'. Reality returns, but for a brief moment the image makers have woven their magic.

There is no doubt that one of the major movements of the last 30 years has been the formation of the image makers. They are everywhere we look. They stand with Tony Blair and William Hague, tell them what to wear, what to say and where to go. They visit the supermarkets we shop in and tell them how best to display the food. They walk with our sporting stars, they create and carry the latest 'pop' sensation. They visit the big manufacturers and tell them what is 'in' and what is definitely 'out'. They are everywhere we turn.

The image makers have a profound effect upon our lives. They can make us feel inadequate unless we purchase a certain product. They manipulate us to believe that one Member of Parliament is more trustworthy than another. They make us believe that there is happiness to be found by living their lifestyle. They convince us that there is no better way to live than theirs. But, worse than this, they now form the very fabric of the society that our children are growing up in. The most dominant shaping force in our children's lives are the image makers. If you are not convinced, let me give you two examples.

Example 1

Your son is a big football fan – every week he sits in front of the television waiting for the results. You go to his room and it is full of his club's merchandise: scarves, posters, games, mugs and so on. When he goes out to play he always wears the same thing – his team's shirt. Enter the image makers with one word – exploitation. So now they weave more of their 'magic' and they design a home and an away strip. Then they decide to change the design of the strips every year. The cost of the shirt is between £40 and £50. And so now the pressure is on – your son has bought into the image. Who can blame him? In order to be 'cool', to be 'in', he needs that new shirt. The old has passed, the new has come. And who does he perceive is stopping him? You! In one 'magical' step the image makers have targeted the little boy and made you the enemy. You can't win. If you don't buy it, you create a barrier between your son and you. If you do buy it, you have given in to the image makers. That is a no-win situation. Hang on in there, though, because later in the book we will look at ways of fighting back.

Example 2

Your daughter is 10 going on 13 and she has just discovered music. Enter the image makers who create an all-girl band – the Spice Girls – to appeal to your daughter. Articles in all the teenage magazines are the first step, interviews on television are the next; thus the machine gets going. Next is sponsorship with a major drinks company – the message to your daughter is 'buy this drink and you will be like the Spice Girls'. This is followed by a whole range of merchandising deals – cosmetics, clothes, even with Asda! Your daughter now wants everything to do with the Spice Girls. And guess what! You've now become the enemy! Not to buy the product creates a barrier between you and your daughter. To buy the product is to give way to the image makers. It is an enormous pressure. Listen to John Toone, Director of Legal and Commercial Affairs at A&M Records:

> No one has more marketability than the Spice Girls ... the girls are like a cartoon, they have become the perfect vehicle.[9]

The image makers are all around us, but I see three major ones.

Image maker 1: The power of advertising

Adverts are now an everyday part of life. We can't move without seeing, hearing or experiencing an advert. Their messages scream to us from boards all over town, in the magazines we buy, on the radio, television, cinema – even the videos that we rent. They've even persuaded us to buy clothes with advertising on them! Walk along any street and you will pass adverts for Boss, Nike, Adidas, Reebok and so on. The ingenuity of advertisers always amazes me. They have created a culture where a small tab on the back of a pair of jeans carries credibility. To have the tab means you are 'in', not to have it – well, you are 'out'. They have achieved this by selling two lies.

LIE 1: BUY THE PRODUCT AND IT WILL MEET SOME DEEP NEED

Adverts primarily work on the basis that purchasing the product will meet some real or perceived need. Take a simple example: I want my clothes to be whiter than white and soft – therefore there is only one soap powder to buy, the one advertised! But it's more subtle than that. A beautiful woman with very few clothes on lies on a bed, her eyes are wide with anticipation, her tongue plays round her mouth. Finally the object of her desire comes into view – an ice-cream! Her tongue now suggestively plays with it. Not a subtle message, but a powerful image. The image? Simple: buy the product – in this case ice-cream – and you will be attractive to the opposite sex.

The power of the advert is that buying the product will satisfy some deep need in us. Take the universal need for acceptance, for example. We all want to be accepted, to be liked, to belong to the group. The image makers have created a culture that has made acceptance dependent on you having their product. If you want to belong to a particular 'group' then you need the right footwear, or the right jeans. I will never forget a chilling moment in a documentary I saw on Nike. The documentary was pointing out that while Nike shoes can cost from £40 to £120 they are mass-produced in the Far East for a very small price. In other words, the company was making a big profit. Then they interviewed some young people in London who had bought the £120 shoes and asked them if they minded that they had been exploited. Their reply was simple and sad: 'Yes, we mind that we have been exploited, but the look is more important and so we'll pay for them.' I find that so sad, for who created the look in the first place? Nike did, or rather the image makers. That is the pressure that is put on our young people.

I remember watching with amusement a mother and daughter having a heated discussion in a major store. The mother had a pair of black jeans in her hand and the daughter had another pair of black jeans. They were 'discussing' which to buy. As far as I could tell, there were only two differences between the pair of jeans; one was price (the mother's pair cost £30 and the daughter's pair £65); the other was the small red label on the £65 pair. It was this that the daughter wanted. These were the jeans all her friends had and so to be part of the crowd, to be accepted, she needed a pair. It was certainly a no-win situation for the mother.

LIE 2: BUY THE PRODUCT AND YOU WILL LOOK THIS GOOD!

I always have difficulty buying clothes as I can never find clothes that match and fit. If the waist fits then the legs are too long. If the legs fit then my backside hangs out. If the legs and my backside fit, then the waist is too big! We often come away from shopping for clothes feeling depressed. Why? Because in the adverts the clothes always fit and look good. But the advert has created a lie. The lie? That these are normal people, with normal body shapes, and if you buy their products you will look just like them.

The reality is very different. The average model in adverts weighs 25% less than the normal person. This is a huge amount – it is unhealthy and impossible to sustain for the vast majority of people. But the image makers create the image that we too can look like that. That is a huge pressure for young people. At an age when they are acutely conscious of their body it is very cruel to bombard them from every direction with these images. They see the advert and think only one thing – failure. They see it and think of better bodies, better clothes and better sex. The advert tells them, be like this and everybody will like you, everybody will love you. But they know it's not possible, and so many feel failures and unloved.

Image maker 2: The power of television and films

Television is a powerful medium which can be used for good and bad. We watch on average 3.5 hours of television a day, which means in one week we watch about 24 hours of television, and that if you live to be 70 you will spend 8 whole years of your life watching television! The question you've got to ask is, 'What images does it create and what influence does it have on my life?'

The debate over the effect television has on our thought and behaviour is big, but I am convinced that television's influence on young people can be great. We need to be so careful about the images they see. Take sex as an example. In films and on television sex is always great. Now don't get me wrong, sex can be great – but there will be difficult times. Most people's first experience of sex is disappointing. The first time can be painful, messy and frankly embarrassing. You never see that in the media. On television and in films it's always silk sheets, warm rooms and everything working perfectly. One word to remember is image. I remember watching a scene from a film when I thought the sink would break. And the angles they get up to – it's just not possible! Always remember image.

Image maker 3: 'you and me' – peer pressure

I remember the day my best mate John told me about the first time he'd had sex with his girlfriend. He was 15. He began to tell me what he'd done with her and as he did so my mouth fell wide open. I could not believe it. The things they'd done were simply amazing, extraordinary. I envied him until the day I got married. Now that I'm married I know my best mate was lying. To have done all he claimed you would need two heads, ten arms and six legs. He made a lot of it up; he created an image. Trouble is, at the time I didn't know any better and believed him. And so I built up this expectation about sex based on what my mates told me. Unfortunately it's an image and it can never be achieved.

That is what we do to one another. You are with five mates. One begins to tell you about the ecstasy pill he'd taken last night. He tells you all the fun he had. A lot of it is true, but the trouble is that you don't get the full picture. He now says he's got some and asks whether you want to take it. Nobody else wants to, but nobody dares say 'no' because there is an image to live up to. To say 'no' is not cool. To say 'no' will mean you are out of the group. That is peer pressure – that is you and me.

That is the power of the image makers, and it is the world which young people are growing up in. We need to stand with them and show them the lies behind all the glossy adverts, the truth about synthetic groans on film and a bit of realism about friends' 'boasting'.

The point is, of course, that advertisers are not interested in our well being; they are interested in our cash. So they are obliged to lie, if not factually, then emotionally and spiritually. Only a fool would believe that a car or a smell really offers happiness and self-fulfilment. But, almost unconsciously, we accept the terms and buy the stuff. When it doesn't work, we don't see the light. We buy more. Such is the imaginative grip of these images. [11]

ACTION POINTS

Stop and think for a moment. Do you unconsciously reinforce the message of the image makers with your children?

You're in the supermarket and for once have a choice of checkouts to queue at. One is operated by a dumpy girl with glasses, the other by a shapely blonde. Which checkout do you join? You think it does not matter, but remember that your children will pick up the hidden message that looks are all that matter.

◆ Positively discriminate in favour of those who are often shunned.

In your circle of friends some will be thin, others overweight. Do you have nicknames for them, like 'rake' or 'fatso', which you think are terms of endearment? What hidden message does it convey to your children, let alone the recipient of the remark? Hidden message: looks are all that matter.

◆ Use positive names for people

Talking about your friend's new girlfriend you say something like, 'I'm sure she's got a nice personality.' Hidden message: looks are all that matter.

◆ Always build people up in public.

Dieting is big business, but you are on a constant diet. Hidden message: looks are all that matter.

◆ Love yourself for who you are, not what you want to be.

A most important page

Having looked at the young people's world and some of the forces that shape it, I hope we are now in a position to move on and discuss ways we can begin to tackle some of the problems. However, before doing that it's important that we understand a vital principle. This book is not full of advice on the types of drugs and their effects, and it's not a sex education manual. There are already plenty of good books on those topics. Rather, in writing this book I've tried to address the underlying principles behind the issues. Statistics and information are vital if we are going to tackle these problems, but there is something more important needed if we want to make real change. And that something is relationships. Before anything can be done about drugs and sex we have to have a relationship with our children. Without that relationship all the statistics and information are worthless because we can't share them. I hope the next few chapters will give you some building blocks to lay a foundation of relationship. If we can maintain a relationship with our children through the good and bad times, then we will have some hope.

So, read on ...

To give them the love they crave for

Imagine that we are sitting in your living-room, talking about your son or daughter, and how you are worried about their friends and the substances they may or may not be sniffing. We talk about the videos they watch and the views they have on sex. We cover most issues about which parents at some point feel out of their depth. In the midst of your confusion I ask you to answer one question: 'What is the most important question on your teenager's mind?'

Take a minute and think about it. What answer would you give? I'm sure lots of questions fly through your mind – exams, career, boyfriends/girlfriends, drugs. All very important questions, but beneath them there is one fundamental question. The young person may never verbalize it or even consciously acknowledge it, but it is there. This is the question: 'Do you love me?'

Deep down inside every son and daughter that question lurks; in a great sense it shapes their whole world. The answer you give to the question is critical both in the way you say it and the manner you say it. When your son is playing his first football match for the school, there is only one person he wants to see on the touchline, and that's you. As your daughter speaks her first line in the school play, there is only one person she wants to see there, and that's you. The desire to be loved and accepted by our parents drives and moulds us – your part in this is crucial.

Let me set you some typical scenes to show you what I mean. It's the end of term, the day your children bring home their school report. Now for all families this is a stressful time and most want to encourage their children in their work. Below are four scenarios where you as parents say one thing which is meant to be encouraging but the young person hears something totally different. In all four scenarios you have just read your son or daughter's reports and these are the conversations that take place.

Scene 1

You say:
'John, we love you, but this report, well, it's just not good enough. I spoke to Sian's parents earlier and she has done so well. Really, John, you can do better.'

John hears:
'I'm not good enough and they wish Sian was their daughter.'

Scene 2

You say:
'John, we love you, but this report – well, frankly, we are a bit disappointed. Your dad never had the opportunities you had and you are blowing it. Now come on, you can do better.'

John hears:

'My parents think I'm a failure and I'll only be a success when I achieve what my dad wanted to be.'

Scene 3

You say:

'Mary we love you, but this report … Now if you want to be a doctor you will have to work much harder. I tell you what, we'll pay you – every A grade you get in the exam we'll give you £10 and every B grade £2.'

Mary hears:

'They are not interested in what I think – I don't want to be a doctor and I don't want their money.'

Scene 4

You say:

'Mary, we love you, let's go out for a coffee and have a chat. Tell me what you think of the report. Do you think it's fair? What lesson do you think we can learn from it?'

Mary hears:

'We love you and value your opinion.'

Now in all four cases the parents love their children and in all four cases the parents acted with the best intentions. The trouble is, we need to understand that the young person is hearing something different from what we are saying. The reason this happens is because we fail to realize that a young person responds very differently from an adult. A young person is behaviourally orientated, whereas adults are verbally orientated. A young person interprets love in terms of behaviour, not primarily in terms of what is said. So when you say 'I love you', which is very important, it needs to be backed up by some action demonstrating that love. So it starts by standing on a football field touchline in the pouring rain and by sitting through the school play. It demonstrates the love they are looking for.

If your behaviour tells the child that you don't love them they will retreat slightly from you. That is very sad because parents are the refuge that young people need. They need a space where they can recharge their emotional batteries. For example, I have a mobile phone and it works well during the day. It has a display board that has a number of indicators. There is a sign that tells me the power of the signal; there is another display that tells me how much life is left in the battery. When it's full the sign says '5', when it's almost empty the sign says '1'. When it's shown '1' for about an hour it begins to bleep – a definite indicator that it is about to 'die'. So before that happens I put the phone in the charger and after about an hour the battery is fully charged and back up to '5'.

In a sense a young person's emotional life is like a mobile phone. It can be anywhere from '1' to '5' but at some point it will need recharging. And the recharging agent is you – the parents. Young people need the love and security of their parents – constantly. And they need it for two reasons:

◆ It helps them to make the transition from childhood to adulthood. It's part of the process of gaining their independence. But to make that step they need the security of a home where they can come back to when they get 'scared'. They go out with the battery full and return with it empty. Part of the responsibility of parenthood is to recharge their batteries.

◆ A young person who knows they are loved and feels secure has more chance of resisting the negative pressures that are 'out there' in the harsh and hard world that our young people are growing up in.

Your child needs to know that you love them unconditionally. That means you love them irrespective of the colour of their hair, their mental, physical and sporting attributes, and their friends. To love them unconditionally means they can grow and explore who they are without worrying about trying to please or fail. It means they develop rounded views on matters. To love them conditionally means they are always looking over their shoulder and are full of anxiety because they never know if they are good enough.

Many teenagers are loved but it's only conditional love – and they know it. Conditional love is based on performance. The teenagers observe that more warmth and love is shown towards them when they achieve certain things: good marks at exams, a position in the rugby team, another grade in the music exams, for example. They have learned that they are valued not for who they are but for what they have achieved. Most parents would be horrified to think it's the way they operate, but sadly it often is. Increasingly in the last 15 to 20 years purely academic success has been perceived as the answer to all problems. Therefore teenagers are put under enormous pressure to pass exams and go on to higher education. There is nothing wrong with that in itself, but it is wrong when the demonstration of love is based on results alone. Certainly with most parents it's not deliberate, but teenagers will pick up any small signals that you give. Encourage them in their studies, support them in their musical and sporting achievements, but love them for who they are, not what they achieve.

I sometimes visit a special needs school. It is a great school with around 120 children with severe disabilities. I visited their assembly on prize-giving day, but this was prize giving of a different kind. The hall was packed with the children and one or two parents who had come to observe what was taking place. I sat at the back next to a 75-year-old woman whom I did not know.

The headmaster began. 'Mary, you have won a prize for holding a knife and fork for the first time.' Mary, a 14-year-old girl, was wheeled forward to collect her prize. As she did so John, a lad with Down's Syndrome standing at the back, applauded her all the way to the front and back again.

'Peter,' went on the headmaster, 'you managed to walk in a straight line this week, come and collect your prize.' As he walked forward, almost in a straight line, John applauded him all the way. This extraordinary celebration of human achievement continued. Prize after prize was given and each time John would applaud the person.

Finally the headmaster said, 'John, you did a good piece of artwork this week, come and collect your prize.'

With that John went to collect his prize and applauded himself! As he went forward, the old woman sitting next to me, who until this point had been very quiet, sat up straight. She nudged me in the ribs and turned to look at me. With a broad smile and tears falling down her face she pointed towards John and simply said, 'That is my grandson.'

I knew nothing about John, but one thing I learned that morning is that he was loved. John has many difficulties and will have many hurdles to overcome in life but one thing is clear – he knows he is loved and that will make all the difference.

Give your child that same demonstration of love – it makes all the difference.

ACTION POINTS

◆ Words are powerful – always use positive ones.

◆ Tell your children you love them, but do more – demonstrate it by your actions.

◆ Spend time with them doing what *they* want to do.

◆ Ask their advice and opinions on issues. Let them see that you value their views by putting some of them into practice.

◆ Respect them as individuals – give them dignity both in private and in public.

◆ Always build them up in front of their friends.

To talk to your son or daughter

 Adam sat in the car next to me. 'Can I ask you a question?' he asked.

'Fire away' I replied.

'Well, it's a bit embarrassing, but John's got this problem – it's not me, you understand,' he said. 'He's got this problem – he's hanging around with his mates and a few of them are smoking cannabis. He can't see what's so wrong with it. What do you think I should say?'

Two things are clear from the conversation. First, John may well have a problem but Adam is the one who can't see anything wrong with smoking cannabis. And secondly, the conversation took place because of the cups of coffee we'd drunk together and the cliffs we'd abseiled together! What I mean by this is that Adam felt he could talk with me not because he'd just met me but, rather, that over the years in the youth club we had spent time together. Time in which he'd worked out if I was trustworthy and if I gave good advice. And the way we got to know each other was by having cups of coffee in our front room and spending days abseiling and canoeing together.

It may surprise you to know that teenagers want to talk about life and their problems. I know that's hard to believe when the most you get out of your children is a monosyllabic grunt – and that's on a good day! But what is more surprising is that the vast majority of young people interviewed said the people they most wanted to talk with were their parents!

So we have a problem – they want to talk with you and you want to talk with them. How come it seems so hard?

Well, I think a couple of ground rules are needed so we can understand what is really going on.

Ground rule 1

You may think that the favours you do – the car runs to band practice or football games – are what your son and daughter are really looking for. Or you may think that the portable CD player you brought for their room really said it all. They are certainly very important and part and parcel of being a parent. However, young people are looking for more than that. They are looking for your undivided time, they are looking for focused attention.

Focused attention is when you give teenagers your total attention and time. It's when you give them *all* your time, you listen to them and you are not distant. This time can be very costly for they often want it when you least can afford to give it. But you must give it if you want to talk with them. So as you are about to fall asleep and you sense the door begin to open, and a voice says, 'Mum, I was wondering ...', you know it's time for focused attention. Or when you've got in from work, you've done all that needs to be done, you open a can of cold beer, collapse into your favourite seat, switch on the TV and as you do so the door opens and your daughter walks in, saying 'Dad ...', you know it's time for focused attention.

Ground rule 2

The older your teenager gets the more time they need with you. Yes, I did say that: the older they get the more time they need. The reason for this is obvious. They are facing more and more dilemmas every day. They are feeling pressure from all quarters – friends, school, society – and they need somewhere where they can take refuge. And that somewhere is you! They need you as a base that they can return to, a sheltered harbour, almost, so that when the storm gets too rough they can head back to you.

Focused attention

What does focused attention do for my children? If we give the right sort of attention it can make all the difference in the world. Focused attention tells young people that they are valued and special. It is the environment that shapes their views and opinions. With the right environment they develop security and confidence in themselves. Without the right input they can become anxious and have a low opinion of themselves. In my time I have met many young people and I can usually put them into two groups: those who have had good focused attention and those who have not. Those who have are often more relaxed with themselves, their body language is open and they mix well with their peers. Those who have not can appear over-confident or withdrawn, anxious and ill at ease with their peers.

SIX TIPS FOR FOCUSED ATTENTION

1 Accept that it is going to take time and be costly to you. It will mean sacrificing some of your space, time and

desires. I recently received a letter from friends whose last child has just left home. They talk about being able to do what they want, watch the videos they choose, go out for a meal when they want. In other words, to give focused time means you give up your desires for the sake of your children.

2 Take the opportunity, because time will pass so quickly. If we listen to our children when they are 5, 6 and 7 there is a chance they will listen to us when they are 15, 16 and 17.

3 Focused attention can be spontaneous, usually at your child's prompting. Most of it, however, is planned by you. It involves getting into a pattern, taking a regular time out in the week to spend alone with your son or daughter. It may be that you go out for a coffee, go shopping, or go to a football match. Whatever you do, it is time that you and your child are alone. They must have your full attention – no mobile phones that may go off, no 'do you mind if we just call in to see Pat, just for a minute', no 'I know we missed last week but I'm under real pressure at work. I promise you I will make it next week.' All these may be valid reasons, but it is not focused time – it's secondary time. It's saying, 'Listen, you are important, but you must fit in with *my* agenda.' That only communicates one thing to the young person: 'I'm not valued'. I know that they may say to you, 'Sure, Dad, I understand, we'll do it next week.' But inside they are dying. You must make the time and stick to it.

4 You will need to give them time to relax. Don't expect that they will talk to you about deep things on your first time. Don't expect that after two months of focused

time that they will sit down with you and unload everything in the first minute you get together. They need time to relax, so go shopping, visit every shop twice! At the end go for a coffee, buy some food, and take your time over it. As you do so they will relax and begin to ask you your opinion.

5 They are asking for your opinion, not a lecture! Try not to look shocked when they share some issues with you, for in sharing they are genuinely looking for some guidance. But it's in this time that you can really talk with them. Share your failures in the past and your worries on issues. As you talk ask them their opinion on the issue and what their friends think. If you are talking about sex and drugs and your teenager's view differs from that of their friends, ask them how they hope to cope and how you can help. You see, this is a conversation of people who respect *each other's opinion*.

6 Pick up the signals for those 'unplanned' focused attention times: when they hang around you for longer than usual, when they begin to talk about something that seems unimportant, when they come into your room late at night. These are critical times, for if we do not recognize them the young person will interpret it as rejection.

As we give young people focused time we are building a haven where they can work out their views away from the pressure of society and peers. But it is also a haven that is created by our views and standards and in that haven we are able to build into young people a framework that will help them cope with all that is 'out there'.

So is communicating with your children really possible? Communication experts talk about five levels of communication that move from the superficial level to the point where intimacy takes place. Here are five questions which illustrate each level.

Level 1	Clichés	'How are you?'
Level 2	Facts	'What did you eat for lunch today?'
Level 3	Ideas	'What do you think?'
Level 4	Feelings	'How does that make you feel?'
Level 5	Transparency	'What is really on your heart?'

Our aim with our children is to create a relationship where level 5 is reached from time to time. I believe that if we give focused attention we have a chance of getting there.

TIME OUT

'My dad says he loves me, but he just never seems to have any time for me.'

'I tried to talk to my mother, but we always end up arguing because she thinks she knows best.'

'I was scared out of my mind at the party. I was so glad when I got home that I could sit on my folks' bed and talk about it.'

'I know my dad's not very cool but at least he always gives me time. Come to think of it, I suppose I'd be lost without him.'

When my dad comes in from work the house fills with laughter.[12]

To help your children think for themselves

One of our ambitions for our children must be that they will learn to think for themselves; that they will think for themselves about the world they live in and the forces that are seeking to shape them. We want them to have the skills and abilities to work out if something is exploiting them or helping them. I'm not talking about an academic ability but rather an inner belief that is developed over years.

On one level we already do this as our children's heads are packed with advice: 'Come straight home from school'; 'Don't accept sweets from strangers'; 'Don't get into a car with somebody you don't know'. These are just some examples of the good advice we give our children. Tragically, we have to teach our children that not everybody in society can be trusted. We are good at that, for it seems that most children listen to the advice.

Teaching our children that all they watch on television is not good for them, however, or that sometimes their mate's advice is bad, or that advertisers don't always tell the truth is *much* harder. How do we make sure that they have the foundation for these things? We have to start by making them think for themselves, encouraging them to become critical thinkers. Now I realize this is hard but it's crucial if we are to give our children any chance of survival. To show you how hard it is let me give you an example from a couple of conversations I have had.

Talking to a colleague the other day, he asked me, 'Did you see the film *Trainspotting*? Well, I …'

But instead of letting him finish I dived in with, 'Yeah, I really enjoyed it. I thought the acting was …'

And as I'm speaking I know, I really know, that he totally disagrees with me. He has watched the same film but we have totally different views about it. Another time I started a conversation with a friend that went something like this. 'I saw an episode of *Cracker* last night. I know there is realism but I do think it's gone too far.' To which my friend replies, 'Oh you're too soft, that's life as we know it.'

Again, the fascinating thing is that we both saw the same programme yet had completely different views on it. And I have deliberately used an issue of censorship to show you how difficult it is for us as adults to know what is good or bad. So how much more difficult will it be for our children? It is crucial that we train our children to think for themselves and become critical thinkers.

To continue with the issue of censorship – in a sense it's a bit like a spectrum where at one end of the line you have child pornography and at the other Disney films such as *Bambi* and *Snow White*.

Child Pornography...**Disney**
We all know it's wrong...It's OK

Now 99.9% of the population agrees that child pornography is wrong and 99.9% agree that Disney type films are innocent. Those are not the problem. The problem lies between the two. That is where the whole issue of censorship lies. For some *Trainspotting* was a powerful film that captured the darkness of modern life, for others it was a film full of swearing. For some, *Cracker* raised real issues, such as rape, in a constructive way, for others it encouraged the rapist. These are big issues. It's hard enough for those of us who are older so what hope is there for young people? Well, there is a lot of hope … but only if we have given them a major weapon. And that is the ability to be a critical thinker.

A critical thinker is somebody who looks at an issue, sees all the arguments and makes a good decision based on the evidence. A critical thinker looks at a film like *Crash* and sees that it's exploitation while a film like *Secrets and Lies* is a great insight into modern life. A critical thinker is able to look at the issues surrounding drugs and alcohol and to realize that they are being exploited by the big national companies that release products like 'Alcopops' with one sole aim – profit. They realize that the only winners in the illegal drugs war are the pushers and dealers. A critical thinker sees beyond our materialistic lifestyle that says money and power are all that count. They see there is more to this life, there are higher ideals to live by.

So how do we get our young people to be critical thinkers? Through hard work over many years! Unfortunately there is no other answer. If there were it would have been packaged and sold! In the next chapter I will give three steps to help us educate our children to think for themselves.

It *is* possible, so read on.

I won't be here in the next century doing this job, but I think there will be a problem; I think our children will be assaulted from all sides; they will have televisions in their room by then, probably video, probably satellite dishes attached to those televisions so they will see everything. We must somehow give them the strength to resist . . . I think it's a matter of survival not only for the individual but also for society.[13]

To know the steps that will help your children think for themselves

As we shared in the last chapter, helping our children to become critical thinkers is a big issue. To help us get the foundation right I will demonstrate how we educate our children to think for themselves, tackling the three major forces we identified as shaping our children's thinking: you and me, advertising and the media.

1. Thinking for themselves about you and me!

We all want our children to become critical thinkers about the pressures their friends will put them under. When their 'mate' offers them a pill at a rave, their ability to say no will be based on foundations you have already set in place. When somebody whispers into your teenager's ear, 'If you love me you'll have sex with me', their answer will be based on the years you have spent educating your child about sex. When a mate asks your daughter to spend an evening helping with a local homeless project their ability to say yes is based on the foundations already set. I have identified three key areas in educating our children to think for themselves in relation to their friends.

A. TEACH THEM THE TRUE VALUE OF MATERIAL POSSESSIONS

As with all things, learning the real value of possessions begins at home and it starts with the kind of lifestyle we portray to our children. If our possessions possess us then this will communicate a message to our children. The message will vary in intensity but the bottom line is that materialism is the answer to all our problems. Don't get me wrong – I believe that material possessions are important. We all need a warm, secure place to live in and food to eat. A car to get us from A to B would be very helpful and a yearly holiday beneficial. But beyond that material possessions do not solve all of life's problems. One of the major problems for young people is that they have seen the shallowness of much of the life we have created. The ability to become critical thinkers begins at home with the foundations we set. And one of the important foundations is to do with our 'attitude' to life. So think about what we are communicating to our children. If we hold lightly to possessions, we demonstrate that, while important, they are not the 'be all and end all' to life.

B. TEACH THEM RIGHT FROM WRONG

An ironic truth about young people is that they say they do not like rules, yet one of the major things they need is boundaries to work within. You will have already learned that children like boundaries because they can explore them! If you say you can do this, but not that, the chance is they will want to do that and not this! If you tell a child not to touch something, they go right ahead and touch it! But in a strange way they find that very secure. Young people want to have boundaries, they want to know what the 'no go' areas are. One of the major roles that is played by parents is teaching their children right from wrong.

It is needed for the security of the child but it is also needed for the well-being of our society. This quote from the *Wall Street Journal* gets to the heart of the issue.

> The United States has a drug problem and a high school sex problem and a welfare problem and an AIDS problem and a rape problem. None of this will go away until more people in positions of responsibility are willing to come forward and explain, in frankly moral terms, that some of the things people do nowadays are wrong.

The ability to recognize right from wrong is learned, primarily, at home.

C. TEACH THEM TO BUILD OTHERS UP, NOT KNOCK THEM DOWN

How we talk about other people in front of our children will determine the way they think and 'criticize' other people. It begins when you come home from work and over the evening meal you are talking about your work colleagues. Maybe most things you say are negative: 'The secretary today, she is so dull. I tell you when God gave brains out He sure forgot her'; 'Mary came back to work today, I have to say I don't see what the boss sees in her. Frankly she's not even pretty'; 'John drove me mad today. He's as thick as two short planks'.

What do you think those comments say to our children? They have passed definite messages to them – that we value people for what they look like, and that secretaries are dull. But above all they have legitimized being negative about people. If running others down in the presence of your children is a regular activity they, too, will grow up with a very negative view of others.

2. Thinking for themselves about the media

The second major influence we looked at was the media. It's essential that we teach our young people to become critical thinkers in this whole area. The point will come, and possibly already has, when your children will want to watch programmes that you feel are not beneficial for them. This is always a point of conflict! How can we tackle the problem? As with all things to do with young people, the issue started when they were much younger and they observed, probably unknown to you, what you watch. In other words, if you think that certain programmes are not helpful to your child you need to have set an example of showing restraint.

So if your life is dominated by the television and you spend hours in front of it you may have problems setting standards with your children. If you constantly hire out '18' rated videos and then try to 'censor' what your child watches do not be surprised if you encounter resistance.

What I suggest is that you need to set certain boundaries early on. When they are young go through the children's television schedule and agree what they can watch and what they can't. I suggest that the amount of time they watch television as well as the content of it is an issue here. You are trying to control not only what they watch but the amount of time they watch it. Then, and this is very important, you need to explain to them *why* they can't watch certain programmes. Tell them what you think is wrong with the content. In this way, you are not censoring in a vacuum; rather, you are explaining why you think it's wrong. In doing this you are helping them to develop a critical mind. It is a mind that questions what it watches; a mind that can differentiate between what is good and what is bad.

Another question to consider is where the television is placed. Does it dominate the room and have all the chairs facing it or is it kept in one corner? In many cases the layout of the room is governed by the position of the TV. If our seating plan is governed by the television it dictates to us our priority – to watch television. If this is the case, change the layout. Have seats facing one another. Place the television in a place that does not dominate the room. Now when you sit in the room you are not automatically looking at the television, but at one another. It may seem a small thing but it really is a major change. If you do this over a period of time your priorities will change.

A final important issue is whether we should allow a television in our child's bedroom. Now obviously there is an age where your teenager can make their own choice, but before that age I believe a television in a child's room is not helpful for three reasons.

First, it is a lot of temptation for them to resist. It is hard enough for us as adults to control what we watch, but it is asking a great deal of a child to have the same restraint. Secondly, you have no control over what they watch. Of course, this may mean that you take your television out of the bedroom to set a good example. Thirdly, and perhaps most importantly, it encourages isolation. The young person will spend more and more time in their room watching the TV, making it more difficult for you to spend time with them.

Finally, you need to be creative. Have the occasional family video night. As a family, get in a pizza and watch a good video together. This will show that you are not against videos or television. In fact, you are for it when there are good things to watch. It also means that you are in control and can choose what you watch.

As the children grow you can begin to watch programmes with them and ask what they think of the content. Ask them what values the programme portrays and whether they are healthy. In this way you are beginning to create in your child a mind that is able to recognize what is good and bad, right and wrong.

Censorship is partly about banning things but it should be more than that. We need to create a positive alternative for teenagers. We need to help them develop critical minds that recognize what is good and bad. That starts with you and me setting the standards.

3. Thinking for themselves about advertising

The final major influence we have looked at is advertising. To help our young people become critical thinkers in this area I want to introduce a game called 'Spot the lie'. This game was created by the writer Os Guinness to play with his son. Christopher was five years old and Os wanted to help him recognize the messages behind the adverts. The rules are simple: parents say 'Spot the lie' when the advert comes on the television. The child has to pay attention and find the implicit lie or totally irrational statement in the advert.

It may be an advert that suggests that if you buy a particular perfume men will fall all over you. It may be that if you buy a certain cigar, peace will descend on your life, or that drinking a certain lager will make you sexy.

In Os Guinness's case, if his son spotted the lie he was given 20 pence. Or you may decide that when they have spotted ten lies you take them to the leisure centre or ten-pin bowling – or any activity that they enjoy doing with the family. However, this is more than a game. This will teach your children to have discernment about life.

Os Guinness was asked whether the game could get expensive. 'Luckily for us,' he said, 'it worked the other way round. Before Christopher bankrupted me, he grew disillusioned with what he was seeing on television. He's 11 now, and he much prefers to read novels and do other things.'[14]

Although 'Spot the lie' is a simple game, one hopes that it encourages young people to see through much of the superficiality of advertising.

Having looked at these three areas, 'you and me', 'the media' and 'advertising', I hope that we can see that there are positive ways forward. It's not just a case of throwing in the towel, but rather of learning how we all can become critical thinkers. Go on, think about it!

ACTION POINTS

◆ Start a weekly TV-free night

◆ Have an agreed list of what the children can and can't watch.

◆ Keep videos and televisions out of the bedroom.

◆ Occasionally, be unpredictable – take your children out on a trip.

◆ Surprise your children – go and offer your help as a volunteer worker with a local hospice, or some similar project.

To remain calm when our worst fears come true

The trouble with writing a book like this is that it may give the impression that there is a simple formula, which, if followed, will mean your children will turn out just how you imagined. Unfortunately, that is not the case, and many parents are sitting at home wondering where they have gone wrong. These are three 'average' situations that will be going on in many homes today.

Scenario 1

Mary's mother can't remember how it started but within half an hour of her daughter coming in from school they were into a full-blown argument. 'Why can't I stay out until two in the morning?' Mary shouted.

'Because you're only 14 and I think it's too late for a girl of your age,' her mother said, trying to keep her rising temper at bay.

'But Amy's mum is letting her stay until then. Oh, please, Mum, it's going to be a great party,' Mary pleaded.

'I'm sorry,' said her mother, 'your father will collect you at 12 o'clock.'

The look on Mary's face said it all. 'My father, my father … he's going to collect me.' The tears came, a look that could kill was given, she turned on her heels, marched to the door and yelled, 'Well, that's it, there's no point in going. You know what, Mum? I hate you.'

The door slammed and the house reverberated to the silence. Her mother sighed and simply thought, 'I'm such a useless parent, where did I fail?'

Scenario 2

John's parents noticed the change in his behaviour about March. Before, his mother described him as a 'pleasant young man'. He mixed well with his mates and was polite to his parents' friends. Around March, though, things started to change. They noticed that he was not eating as usual, nothing startling, but just a change in pattern. Then when he came home from school he no longer went to the kitchen to make some toast and then collapse in front of the television, but instead would go straight up to his bedroom and stay there until he went out again. At first they put this down to adolescence and his 'growing pains'. But his behaviour began to change. Some days he was fine, other days he was miserable and would not give anyone the time of day. It was the money that finally made them take action. At first, John's parents had argued about it, convinced one of them had lost the £100. Both were certain it was left in the usual place, the tin in their bedroom. They got over that, but when the following month another £85 went missing they finally realized what was going on.

When they confronted John, he said nothing. He just sat in his chair looking at them and through them. Finally he just got up and walked out the door. John's parents knew it was against everything they believed but they had to search his bedroom. It was his father who discovered them, in a little tin under all his clothes. As he opened the tin, his heart went icy cold. Inside were a small syringe, a razor blade and mirror. The parents stood looking at these alien objects and simply wondered, 'How have we failed? Where did we go wrong?'

Scenario 3

Joy simply told her mother on Wednesday night, 'Mum, I don't know how to tell you this ... but I'm pregnant.'

Silence hung in the air for a few moments and for a couple of seconds Joy kept her head up in some sort of defiance. But then the weeks of worry took their toll. The first missed period. 'Oh, it's probably one of those things,' her friend had told her. But then there was a second missed period, then the sickness and finally the test. At first her boyfriend swore he would stick with her, but lately he seemed to be avoiding her. As she stood defiantly facing her mother, all her energy seemed to evaporate, she started to sniffle, then to cry and finally just sobbed and sobbed and sobbed. Her mother ran to her daughter and held her tightly. For now her daughter needed her. The questions – 'Where did we go wrong? How did we fail?' – would come later.

These stories show two things. First, it is true that being a parent can be very painful. Secondly, parent after parent will at some time express the sentiment; 'Where did we go wrong? How did we fail? How can we cope with this?' These are big issues and there are no simple answers. There will be pain, tears and sleepless nights before it's all over. But one thing is very clear: at some point we must put the past behind us and move on. Whatever has happened, whatever pain has been inflicted, it must be dealt with. If this step is not taken a wall will be built between you and your children which will go with them into adulthood. It will affect your whole relationship and so my advice is that you deal with it. And the only way to move on is by dealing with the issues. There are four important things we need to realize to help us move on.

A. YOU ARE NOT ALONE

I have listened to many parents explain to me the problems they are having with their children. They go through a whole catalogue of issues. But what becomes clear is that they think their circumstances are so unusual that if other people somehow found out they would be treated like lepers. The truth is that no family is excluded from difficulties. Whatever you are going through right now, please understand that thousands of other people are in the same position. Now I know that does not solve the problem, but it certainly helps to know you are not alone. It helps to know that your children are normal and that every other parent is pulling their hair out as well!

B. DON'T BLAME YOURSELF

One thing is certain about children: there are no guarantees. You can read all the books, follow all the guidelines, do everything right and still find that they do things you wish they hadn't. Human nature is such that two siblings can be totally different. The first child is easy going, he slept through the night, played well with other children and now, as he's growing up he listens to his parents' advice. When the second child was born, the parents repeated all the same processes but this time the child was fractious, slept badly, mixed poorly and is now refusing to do what he's told. So if your children do not turn out how you hoped you can't blame yourself!

There is also not much point in blaming yourself because even if you have made some mistakes you can't rewind the clock. You can't dwell on the past because you can't go back. However, to move on you must deal with the past. The next chapter deals with this whole issue so hang on until we get there.

C. WHERE WILL THEY GO IF WE DON'T SUPPORT THEM?

If, for whatever reason, we withdraw our love and support from our children, we have created a worst-case scenario. First, we have withdrawn our love and support when they most need it, and secondly, they will probably be at the mercy of the culture against which we are trying to help them stand.

As an example of what I mean, let me tell you about David. He was a bright lad who had lived on the streets for over two years. He made a living by begging, stealing and occasionally selling his body. He moved from hostel to hostel in search of a place he could call 'home'. When I asked him about his parents, his answer was stark and simple – they did not want him. As he talked his story unfolded. He was an average teenager growing up at home with all the usual hassles. At some point he began to hang out with a group of lads that his parents called 'undesirable'. At first his parents used to argue with him about them. Then they began to tell him what he could and could not do. For example, his friends were not welcome in the house and they did not want to see them hanging around outside. Then his parents returned early one night to discover his friends in the house. A number of them were drunk and one was smoking an illegal substance. It was the last straw for his parents. They gave him an ultimatum: his family or his mates. It wasn't much of a choice, really. He left within ten minutes.

'Why don't you give them a call?' I asked. I will never forget his words, 'I have and they always hang up when they know it's me.'

Now I realize that his is an exceptional case but it highlights the point. If you withdraw your support, where will your children get it from? They need your love and support. However painful, deal with the past and move on with them.

D. IT'S TRAGIC – BUT PUT IT INTO CONTEXT

I have a number of friends whose children have died in tragic circumstances. It is painful and heartbreaking. However, if there is anything positive to be learned from the experience, it's that it puts life in perspective. Poor reports, disappointing exam results and a controversial choice of friends may all be a bit of a let-down for you as a parent, but do keep things in perspective. Discovering that your son has got somebody pregnant, or that your daughter is pregnant is devastating news – it will change your life – but they still have their health, and they still have their life before them. Keep things in perspective.

So how do you move on? What is the key to putting the past behind you and moving on together with your children? I will deal with that in the next chapter. Before that I would like you to read an old story that has been re-written by the American writer, Philip Yancey.

A young girl grows up on a cherry orchard just above Traverse City, Michigan. Her parents, a bit old-fashioned, tend to overreact to her nose ring, the music she listens to, and the length of her skirts. They ground her a few times, and she seethes inside. 'I hate you!' she screams at her father when he knocks on the door of her room after an argument, and that night she acts on a plan she has mentally rehearsed scores of times. She runs away.

She has visited Detroit only once before, on a bus trip with her church youth group to watch the Tigers play. Because the newspapers in Traverse City report in lurid detail the gangs, the drugs, and the violence in down-town Detroit, she concludes that is probably the last place her parents will look for her. California, maybe, or Florida, but not Detroit.

Her second day there she meets a man who drives the biggest car she's ever seen. He offers her a ride, buys her lunch, arranges a place for her to stay. He gives her some pills that make her feel better than she's ever felt before. She was right all along, she decides: her parents were keeping her from all the fun.

The good life continues for a month, two months, a year. The man with the big car – she calls him 'Boss'– teaches her a few things that men like. Since she's underage, men pay a premium for her. She lives in a penthouse, and orders room service whenever she wants. Occasionally she thinks about the folks back home, but their lives now seem so boring and provincial that she can hardly believe she grew up there.

She has a brief scare when she sees her picture printed on the back of a milk carton with the headline 'Have you seen this child?' But by now she has blonde hair, and with all the make-up and body-piercing jewellery she wears, nobody would mistake her for a child. Besides most of her friends are runaways, and nobody squeals in Detroit.

After a year the first sallow signs of illness appear, and it amazes her how fast the boss turns mean. 'These days, we can't mess around,' he growls, and before she knows it she's out on the streets without a penny to her name. She still turns a couple of tricks a night, but they don't pay much, and all the money goes to support her habit. When the winter blows in she finds herself sleeping on metal grates outside the big department stores. 'Sleeping' is the wrong word – a teenage girl at night in downtown Detroit can never relax her guard. Dark bands circle her eyes. Her cough worsens.

One night as she lies awake listening for footsteps, all of a sudden everything about her life looks different. She no longer feels like a woman of the world. She feels like a little girl, lost in a cold and frightening city. She begins to whimper. Her pockets are empty and she's hungry. She needs a fix. She pulls her legs tight underneath her and shivers under the newspapers she's piled atop her coat. Something jolts a synapse of memory and a single image fills her mind: of May in Traverse City, when a million cherry trees bloom at once, with her golden retriever dashing through the rows and rows of blossomy trees in chase of a tennis ball.

God why did I leave home, she says to herself, and pain stabs at her heart. *My dog back home eats better than I do now*. She's sobbing, and she knows in a flash that more than anything else in the world she wants to go home.

Three straight phone calls, three straight connections with the answering machine. She hangs up without leaving a message the first two times, but the third time she says, 'Dad, Mom, it's me. I was wondering about maybe coming home. I'm catching a bus up your way, and I'll get there about midnight tomorrow. If you're not there, well, I guess I'll just stay on the bus until it hits Canada.'

It takes about seven hours for a bus to make all the stops between Detroit and Traverse City, and during that time she realizes the flaws in her plan. What if her parents are out of town and miss the message? Shouldn't she have waited another day or so until she could talk to them? And even if they are home, they probably wrote her off as dead long ago. She should have given them some time to overcome the shock.

Her thoughts bounce back and forth between those worries and the speech she is preparing for her father. 'Dad, I'm sorry. I know I was wrong. It's not your fault; it's all mine. Dad, can you forgive me?' She says the words over and over, her throat tightening even as she rehearses them. She hasn't apologized to anyone in years.

The bus has been driving with the lights on since Bay City. Tiny snowflakes hit the pavement rubbed worn by thousands of tires, and the asphalt steams. She's forgotten how dark it gets at night out here. A deer darts across the road and the bus swerves. Every so often, a billboard. A sign posting the mileage to Traverse City. *Oh God*.

When the bus finally rolls into the station, its air brakes hissing in protest, the driver announces in a crackly voice over the microphone, 'Fifteen minutes, folks. That's all we have here.' Fifteen minutes to decide her life. She checks herself in a compact mirror, smoothes her hair, and licks the lipstick off her teeth. She looks at the tobacco stains on her fingertips, and wonders if her parents will notice. If they're there.

She walks into the terminal not knowing what to expect. Not one of the thousand scenes that have played out in her mind prepare her for what she sees. There, in the concrete-walls-and-plastic-chairs bus terminal in Traverse City, Michigan, stands a group of forty brothers and sisters and great-aunts and uncles and cousins and a grandmother and great-grandmother to boot. They're all wearing goofy party hats and blowing noise-makers, and taped across the entire wall of the terminal is a computer-generated banner that reads 'Welcome home!'

Out of the crowd of well-wishers breaks her Dad. She stares out through the tears quivering in her eyes like hot mercury and begins the memorized speech, 'Dad, I'm sorry. I know ...'

He interrupts her. 'Hush, child. We've got no time for that. No time for apologies. You'll be late for the party. A banquet's waiting for you at home.' [15]

Go on, life's too short ... take the first step.

When I was a boy of fourteen, my father was so ignorant I could hardly stand to have him around. But when I got to twenty-one, I was astonished at how much the old man had learned.
Mark Twain

'Why don't you give your parents a call?' I asked. I will never forget his reply: 'I have and they always hang up when they know it's me.'

It may be a disaster, but is it the end of the world?

To deal with the past and move on

So how do we deal with the past? How do we deal with the pain of perceived failure? As I hope we have already seen there are no simple answers. But I am certain of one thing: to be able to move on we will at some point have to say these three words: '*I forgive you*'.

Three simple words; yet I have long come to the conclusion that they are probably the most dynamic in the world. The power that forgiveness carries is enormous, for when these three words are uttered, no matter how hesitantly or quietly, they bring healing into broken and disturbed lives. Forgiveness can reach down into the darkest hole and release you from years of anguish and pain. In short, they must be three of the most powerful words in the world.

Tragically the opposite is also true, for I have seen life after life that has been ruined because people would not forgive, they would not leave the past behind. For those who will not forgive, a power takes over their existence. Like a cancer it slowly spreads and affects every part of their life. It eats away at the very core of their being. It governs the way they respond to many different issues.

And time makes no difference. Years after an event you just have to say the wrong words and it touches a raw nerve and the person erupts.

At some point in your role as parent you are going to fail, and you are going to be failed by your children. A wrong word will be said, a wrong action will be done, and unintentionally hurt will be inflicted. It *will* happen. What you must decide is how you are going to respond. Will you bottle it up inside and feel that you are not appreciated, or will you confront it, deal with the past and bring the healing power of forgiveness? If you do that you can then move on together with the slate wiped clean. It's your choice.

However, it is also my observation that we find 'I forgive you' incredibly hard words to say. And the longer we leave it, the harder it gets. So what is it that stops us forgiving one another? Below I've listed the four enemies of forgiveness.

Enemy number 1: we don't know how to say it

This could well be the biggest enemy of forgiveness. Although they are only three simple words, they are so hard to get out. When is the best time to say it? Where is the best place? How do I start the conversation? Let me give you a hint from something I do that I find very helpful. Sometimes I sense that something is not right with my wife or friends. Now I know that it could be a number of things but I'm just not certain, so I try using a very simple line: 'Tell me, are you OK, or is there something wrong?' What that has done is opened the door to communication. If I have offended them without realizing it then they can reply, 'Well, actually, now that you mention it …', and they are off – they tell me how when I said something to them last week I really upset them. So now I can say, 'Listen, I'm really sorry, I didn't realize I'd hurt you. I'm really sorry, will you forgive me?' Before we know it we've hit the three words and everything is out in the open.

At other times I've tried a more direct approach with the following types of words. 'Listen, there may be nothing in this, so just ignore me if I've got this wrong, but you do seem a bit cool towards me and I'm wondering if I've done something wrong.' Again, a door is open and they can say a number of things. 'Oh no, I'm just a bit preoccupied at the moment. Things are a bit hard at work and my mind's on that. Thanks for asking but really, everything is OK.' Alternatively, they may say, 'Yes, I am a bit cool and it just goes to show how insensitive you are. How could you not notice the way you treated me last week? What you did made me feel so small.' At which point we would get into a long conversation, during which the person is able to sound off. After some time the point will come when I say, 'Listen, it was stupid of me and I'm really sorry. Will you forgive me?'

Now I realize that with young people life is often not that straightforward and a direct question does not always get a direct answer! However, most of us are normally aware if we have said something that has caused hurt and the solution is that we need to apologize for it.

A reason why we may not want to do that, however, is deadly enemy number 2.

Enemy number 2: pride

Pride is common to all of us. There is a right sort of pride – pride in a son or daughter who does well, pride in a piece of work that you have done, pride in your country. But there is another, darker side to pride, a pride that always puts 'me' first, a pride that holds the chin out and the head up. As an example, see if you recognize yourself in any of these statements:

◆ How dare they say that to me? Who do they think they are?

◆ Forgive them – never! What they did to me was unforgivable.

◆ I'm not going to them. It's their problem. If they come and see me and sort it out, then fine. But until then I'm not doing anything.

◆ I don't care if she is 17, she had no right to do what she did!

Recognize any of them? For *any* relationship to work there has to be give and take. We have to recognize that we can be, and are – at times – wrong. We have to admit that other people may be, and are – from time to time – right. Equally we need to recognize that there will be times when our children are right and we are in the wrong.

To admit that you are wrong and have made a mistake is not a sign of weakness, it is actually a healthy sign. Don't let something remain unresolved for the simple reason that you think you will lose face if you admit to a mistake. Far from it: you will grow in stature in front of your children. Children and young people do not see your admission of past failures as a weakness. Rather, they see it as a bridge that they can walk across to meet you. A shared failure makes us much more approachable and really helps our children.

Enemy number 3: we enjoy the pain!

It may seem strange, but my observation of relationships is that within all of us there is a martyr complex. There are times when we enjoy wallowing in self-pity. We feel that nobody understands us, everything is conspiring against us and in our minds we have arguments with everyone. So if your partner has done you wrong, in your mind you begin to imagine all the things you would like to say to them – and you enjoy it. The trouble with some people is that it goes another step and they actually take on the personality of a martyr. How do you recognize them? Well, every time you meet them they always talk negatively about other people. They never have a kind word to say about someone. They may start the sentence with a statement such as, 'I saw Jane the other day, she looks quite good.' If they left it there it wouldn't be too bad but there is always a but: 'but so would I if I had all her money. Do you know, life is *so* unfair. It's all right for her. Mind you, I would do what she does …'; and so the conversation goes.

There are some people who enjoy the pain. Who knows where or when it began. But what is certain is that at some point in the past somebody has done or said something and they have not sorted out the hurt. They have let it gather dust and now it drives their whole life. The funny thing, in a sad way, is that if you ask them what the hurt was they would not know. It has got so buried with everything else.

If you have got into such a category, break out of it. Stop being negative, talk to the people who have upset you, and bring forgiveness into your life.

Enemy number 4: too much time has passed

A comment that is often made to me by parents goes something like this. 'We've really loved our kids, but looking back there are some things we now wish we had done differently. But they are 22 now and it's too late. If we could turn the clock back 14 years, who knows? I suppose we have to live with it.' Well, yes and no. Yes, you can't turn the clock back but no, it's not too late.

I've lost count of how many times it's been said that: 'Time heals'. Well, for some things it does – a cut leg heals in time, the immediate pain of the loss of a loved one gradually becomes easier to bear. But time does not heal the pain of a wrong word or action. All time does is build a hard layer over the pain, and if somehow that layer is pierced it is still raw underneath. It's never too late to say the words 'I'm sorry'.

So if you feel you've failed your children and they are now 22, sit them down and tell them. Say you are really sorry – it will be like a new beginning. No matter how many years have passed it is never too late to tell somebody you forgive them.

All of us fail and we will all be let down. That is not the issue here. The issue is how do we deal with it, and move on.

Put it right today. You know it makes sense.

ACTION POINTS

◆ Build those bridges for your children to walk over.

◆ If you know you've hurt somebody, put it right – today.

◆ If your son or daughter has hurt you, put it right – today.

◆ You are never too old to say, 'I'm sorry'.

◆ It's better to get it wrong and make a fool of yourself than live the rest of your life with regret.

The first, and often the only, person to be healed by forgiveness is the person who does the forgiving.

Drugs were an escape for me. They removed my feelings of insecurity, fear and inadequacy. I didn't know it, but I needed to be surrounded by security and love. All my life I had tried to buy love. I always pretended that I had it.

STATS THAT SAY A LOT

In an average school of 1000 children, 700 will be offered drugs at some point:

90 will try ecstasy.
200 will try amphetamines.
300 will try cannabis.

Smoking kills six times more people in the UK than road and other accidents, murder, manslaughter, suicide, illegal drugs and AIDS all put together.

Most adult smokers started before they were 18.

In a survey, 10% of 14–15 year olds said they got drunk once a week.

1000 people under 15 are admitted to hospital every year with acute alcohol poisoning.

Only 1 in 7 young people aged between 13 and 15 thinks that sex outside of marriage is wrong.

In an average lower-sixth form of 180, at least 90 will be sexually active.

Only 25% thinks under age sex is wrong.

Only 20% thinks there is anything wrong with divorce.

To help your children stay drug free

Mary sat in the office and told me her story. I was moved and just wanted to cry, because while Mary's story is unique to her it is also tragically true of thousands of other young people.

'I was 12 and hanging around with a group of girls,' Mary began. 'We were no different from anybody else – just out for a good time. One day one of the girls produced a bottle from her schoolbag. I knew what it was because my dad had one back home – it was whisky. She took a swig from the bottle and turned to Claire. I still can see the fear in Claire's eyes. Should she take it or not? She grabbed the bottle, took a swig and coughed it all up. We all laughed and it sort of helped in the wrong way. Jo was next to Claire and so the bottle did the round, until it came to me. You see, Paul,' she continued 'I knew the dilemma. I really did not want to drink it, but everybody already had. For me not to drink it would have made me out to be a dork, a wimp – I would be out of the group. These were my friends and I did not want to lose them, so I took a drink. For me that was the beginning of the end. A year later, when I was 13, I was drinking a bottle of Jack Daniels a day and by the time I was 14 I was mainlining heroin.'

She continued, 'At first it was a bit of fun, but that soon changed. My life went out of control. I began to suffer from anxiety attacks and paranoia. I made my mother's life a misery. My life was hell.' When I asked her why she had taken that first drink, she replied, 'That's simple – they were my friends and I did not want to lose them.'

Drugs and alcohol abuse are major problems in our modern culture. They are among the issues that create great fear and concern for parents. Images of your child connected to a life-support machine haunt the mind. Parties where you have no idea what is going on and what is being given out. How can we ensure that our children remain drug free? How can we create a framework that gives our children the best opportunity to stand against the tide and say 'no' to drugs? It will be hard and there are no easy answers but we need to make a start. We need to have a better understanding of the reasons why young people take drugs, and below is a list of some of them.

Reasons why young people take drugs

◆ To rebel or shock people.

◆ So that they feel that they belong to a group of friends.

◆ Because they want to take risks.

◆ Because it's fun.

◆ Because it's the in thing to do.

◆ It's part of a night out – maybe at a rave.

◆ Because it feels and looks grown-up.

◆ It's an escape from the pressures of living in modern society.

◆ Because they're bored.

◆ Because drugs are easy to get hold of.

All of the above are reasons why young people take drugs but there is a fundamental reason which we need to get hold of and understand. Young people – or anybody for that matter – take drugs because they work. Drugs work, they give a buzz, they *do* make you feel good. If drugs did not work people would not take them. Thousands of people die every year because they smoke tobacco. If smoking did not work would people take that risk? Of course not – they take the risk because smoking works for them, they don't think that any of the major health risks will happen to them.

Ecstasy works for the young person. They go to a rave and they pay their £15, take the pill and have a good time. So please understand: drugs work.

There is also another angle that we need to understand. Paul is 14 and every day that he goes into school, it starts: the words that hurt, the push in the corridor, the written notes on his desk. Paul is the victim of bullying and his life is in pain. Sarah is 15 and her GCSEs are six months away. She is slowly suffocating at the pressure of expectation and her life is in pain. Mary hates going home because either her parents are continually arguing, or a heavy silence fills the place. The house feels dark and sinister. She loves her mother and she loves her father, and at the moment she feels as if she is being pulled in two directions and her life is in pain. At some point for any of these young people somebody may come along and whisper into their ears, 'For £20 I can take the pain away – just try one of these'. And they take the pill and for a while the pain goes away. The drug has worked.

Of course we all know that there is another side to the story. No alcoholic ever had one drink and said, 'I'm going to become an alcoholic.' No, the first drink led to a second that led to a third and it began. No junkie who ever started on cannabis said, 'I'm going to become a junkie'. Rather, they tried one substance and when the 'buzz' faded they tried a bit more and when that 'buzz' failed they moved on to another substance. And so before they knew it they were addicted. The ecstasy-popper at the rave did not say, 'I'm going to spend the night in hospital'. But they took it, a great thirst overcame them, their head began to spin and breathing was difficult. Before they knew it they were racing through the streets of the town in the back of an ambulance.

How can we keep our children drug free? How can we prepare our children to say 'no' to drugs and 'yes' to a drug-free lifestyle? Well, it begins by recognizing three truths:

TRUTH 1
Does my son or daughter know that I love them unconditionally, with no strings attached?

TRUTH 2
What messages am I sending to my children? If I come home and I have a couple of whiskies to unwind I won't stand much chance if I tell my children not to take drugs. It goes back to one of the major issues we looked at earlier. Saying 'we love you' is important but it must also be backed up by consistent behaviour that reinforces the statement. The above scenario is not consistent.

TRUTH 3

To be able to help our children we need to be informed about the types and effects of drugs that are around. Pick up any Health Authority leaflet on the subject; you should find one in your doctor's surgery, in your local library or if your child is in school ask them for one.

So how do we win the battle with this issue? Below I have set out eight steps which I believe will lay a foundation that can give us hope.

Eight steps that can help your child stay drug free

STEP 1

Recognize that no area of Britain is untouched by drugs and that the children in your son's or daughter's school can get anything they want. If we fail to accept this it will be very hard to tackle the problem. We have to face up to the reality of the wide and easy availability of drugs.

STEP 2

Have a cup of coffee with your daughter or son and talk with them about the issues. Now please note I said *with* them not *to* them. To help you with what to say and how to say it, these are some of the comments that are made by young people who have attended one of our presentations on drug abuse. Notice what they say for it tells you what they need.

◆ Very honest and open.

◆ The speaker treated us as adults and was not patronizing.

◆ I wish you would say more about peer pressure and how to fight it.

◆ He gave us the facts but let us make the choice – it was good.

What these young people are saying is that they want openness, honesty and all the facts, so that's where you must start. Don't say 'Listen, honey, I know you think we are old and out of touch but we know that drugs are bad and don't work. We love you so please don't do it.' What she thinks is, 'You are right, you are old and out of touch because I know drugs are fun'. Rather, you begin, 'I understand that it's hard with all your mates. And I know they seem to have a good time, but tell me what you know about drugs, tell me what you've learned.' In this way your discussion has started and the lines of communication are open.

STEP 3
As you talk with your son or daughter explain what your views are on drugs and alcohol. Tell them how you set your standards for drinking, and what you think is an acceptable level for you. Share with them how you came to that conclusion.

STEP 4
If you are taking regular medication (which is a different issue) share why you take it. If you lecture your children on drugs while at the same time regularly take prescribed drugs they get the message that one rule is for them, and one rule is for you.

STEP 5

Do you have drink at home? Explain to them why. What is your policy on them drinking alcohol with you? Again, explain why.

STEP 6

As you talk the issues through with your children, gently share with them your views on the topic. Share your concerns about excessive alcohol and drug abuse. Try not to get into lecturing mode!

STEP 7

Tell them the good news. While everybody talks about the number of young people who take drugs remind them that over 70% say 'no' to drugs. Talk to them about how they can learn to say 'no'. Share with them how they can cope with the friends who may be pressurizing them to take drugs. As we know, one of their fears will be that if they say 'no' to their friends they will be excluded from the group. Explain that saying 'no' means they are in the majority, and that they will be still part of the 'in' crowd. It may also be a good time for them to learn that true friends stick with you, and don't desert you when the going gets tough.

STEP 8

Keep your home open to their friends. Let them know they are always welcome, no matter what they look like! If you exclude their friends you are placing barriers between you and your children. To exclude their friends communicates only one thing to your children: you don't love them. To have an open door to your children's friends also means you have some idea of what is going on. But remember, I only said *some* idea!

It is a big issue, but we can make a difference. Go on, keep trying!

1 Don't panic. It will be hard, because everything inside you will want to panic as you'll feel out of control. Hang on in there, for there *is* help!

2 Love them. Whatever you may be feeling at the moment the most important thing your child needs is your love and support.

3 Talk to someone about the situation, tell them how you feel. You will need support through the situation.

4 Get help for your child. There are many good agencies around. Talk to your doctor, a social worker or your child's teacher for advice on who to go to.

5 Realize that all of this will take time. The problem is not going to be solved overnight. You are looking for gradual changes. Hang on in there – a better day *is* coming.

6 Don't blame yourself. You have not failed – it is sadly a part of the young people's world.

ACTION POINTS

◆ Pick up a Health Education leaflet on drug, alcohol and substance abuse from your local surgery or library.

◆ Take some time this week to sit and listen to your child's view on drugs.

◆ If you haven't met your children's friends let them know they are very welcome in your home.

◆ Don't scare your children with shock tactics – it doesn't work.

◆ Check with your children's school on their drug policy. Find out what they are teaching.

◆ If your local school puts on a drugs information evening for parents – go to it. Find out all you can.

I didn't know how I'd react when I discovered my daughter was taking drugs, I wasn't prepared for this. Would I be angry – like you are with a four-year-old who gets lost in the supermarket and you spank them out of fear when you find them? But when I saw her I just held her close and cuddled her and she cried. I didn't judge her, all that mattered to me was that she should survive and know that whatever she did and whatever happened, I'd be there for her.[16]

greatest fears people
...ay are the fear that they
...oved and the fear that they
...e able to love. People are
...meaningful, intimate, lasting
re...onships. I don't believe we've had
a sexual revolution, I believe we have
experienced a revolution in search of
intimacy.[17]

To get sex in its right place

Men apparently think about sex every six seconds. It strikes me that figure is wrong if we take a close look at our world. Everything in our society tells us that *all* we ever think about is sex. You can't open a magazine, walk past an advertising hoarding, go to the cinema, walk into a shop or hire a video without being bombarded by some sexual image. It is all around us. It is enormous pressure because as we have already seen it creates an image of sex that is far removed from reality.

But if it puts enormous pressure on us, imagine what it does for young people. They see an image of a model and think that is what we are meant to look like. As the actress plays her part many an adoring fan watches the big screen and wishes for her looks. A young couple go to see a film and 20 minutes into it the actors begin their sexual routine. It's all so wonderful – for a start, the bed is always made! They appear very confident, they both smell lovely with no hint of body odour, and finally they both know what to do and where to put everything. They reach climaxes together and lie contentedly in each other's arms afterwards. The young people watching the film come to the conclusion that sex is simple and easy to master. They are about to discover the reality that it can be messy and devastating.

Sex can be and is great, but there is a learning experience. Whenever I speak to young people I try to tell them my honeymoon story because I think it gives a 'balanced' view that the media never portrays. This is what happened to my wife and I on our wedding night.

When we finally got to the hotel it was eleven o'clock at night. It looked smaller than it had appeared in the brochure and I felt my heart sink. Just about the only contribution I'd made to the wedding arrangement was to choose the hotel. The day had gone well and my wife was looking radiant. I so wanted the evening to be memorable. We found our room and it was lovely, and Jane smiled when she saw the chilled bottle of wine and roses on the bed. I began to relax, everything was going to be great.

And it could have been, but to my horror I noticed that there wasn't a double bed but two singles. I quickly found the manager. 'This is our honeymoon, and this is meant to be your honeymoon suite!' I said.

The manager was very apologetic but explained that due to an oversight another couple were in the honeymoon room and were well settled.

'But there are single beds in here,' I pleaded. At that point I should have argued and demanded my rights. But when the manager suggested a solution I went along with it as he said it had worked before.

'I'll send you up some rope,' he said 'and you can tie the beds together.'

'Send it up fast!' I exclaimed.

And so on the night I'd waited 28 years for, the night I'd long dreamed of, I was giving it my best effort when the beds parted. Jane and I both crashed to the floor. I looked up at the ceiling and wanted to die, but just then Jane leant over and whispered into my ear, 'Darling … I think I felt the earth move.' The laughter could be heard long into the night.

Jane and I have moved on from there. Sex is great but it's a learning curve that involves laughter, tears, and misunderstandings. Why? Because sex is part of a relationship. One of the big lessons you can teach your children is exactly that – sex is not just a biological act, it's much deeper than that. We need to place it in the context of worth, value and love. High ideals, I realize, but that's what young people are looking for.

Simply the best

When it comes to the issue of sex one thing is very obvious: you need to decide what you believe is right and communicate that to your children. If you are married, both partners need to agree and say the same thing!

For me, I believe the right place to enjoy sex is in a lifelong relationship – in marriage. I believe with all my heart that's what's best for me, for our young people, and for all of us. I know many will not agree with me but that's where I start from. It may be that you do not agree with me and that you are happy for your children to have sex outside marriage when they are over the legal age. My advice to you is simple: give them all the information that they need so that they can make informed choices.

Why do I believe that sex is best reserved for marriage, despite the fact that so many marriages break down? I believe in a life-long commitment because I know of no better model that works. I know of no better model for bringing a sense of intimacy and security to one another.

I know of no better model for bringing children up. It is a theme that occurs throughout the world.

I also believe that all the medical evidence points to the fact that the greatest protection from sexually transmitted diseases is when we stick with one partner, who is not infected, for life. As I write this book, health organizations are having to rewrite the book about HIV and AIDS. It has become a global epidemic with an estimated 20 million people infected with HIV, and a projected 40 million by the year 2000.

I believe that a life-long relationship is the best place to have sex because it can be learned together, in security. You can share in a secure emotional environment. I believe that is the best for humanity and what I want our children to experience.

So now let us move on and look at what, when and how to talk about sex.

Without exception, young people wanted their parents to talk to them about sex.[18]

To know what, when and how to talk about sex

What parents have not watched their 15-year-old daughter get dressed for a party and not worried about the unknown? Which parent has not worried as their 16-year-old son walks off into the night with his mates? How can we best help our young people in the whole area of sex and sexuality? How can we help them to stay as young and innocent, yet wise, as possible? These are some of the questions I hope to answer in the next few pages.

I have many vivid memories of growing up! One of the most disturbing was when I began to notice an alarming change had taken place within me. Up to a certain age I thought that girls were smelly, awful and a pain to have around. But almost overnight my perception of them changed – alarmingly, I began to change my opinion of them. Frankly, they had become very attractive and nice. But worse still was that before this day I was very confident with the girls, and after this day I became a bungling fool. When I was with them I did not know what to say, and – even worse – I just wasn't sure what they thought of me. They were glorious days and they were painful days. They were the days of growing into adolescence.

The reason I share this with you is that we often forget what it was like to be a teenager. We forget the passions that raged in our bodies, we forget the disturbing thoughts and the fear of rejection. We forget the mood swings and the fluctuating desires for independence and the need to come home. We must remember what it was like, because if you have teenagers this is exactly what your son and daughter are going through.

Lessons in sex education

A. DON'T PANIC!

A number of things will begin to happen when your children begin to move from being children to young adults. These are a few of them, in no particular order:

◆ Your food bill begins to rocket.

◆ Their body grows inches in months.

◆ Spots appear all over their face.

◆ One day they act responsibly, the next they act like an 8-year-old.

◆ Hormones come alive.

◆ The opposite sex is discovered.

These are the signs of the teenage years, and the time they need clear guidelines on sex.

B. COMMON BELIEFS

As I shared in the previous chapter, if you have a partner then you have to decide what you both think is acceptable and what is not. You then have to agree to say the same thing. It will be no good if one of you says, 'I know Dad says that, but ...' or 'Don't worry, son, I'll have a word with Mum, just be careful'. You need to have a consistent policy. If you agree with my perspective that sex is best reserved for a life-long relationship, then you need to work out your reasons for this and explain them to your children. If you don't agree you need to decide what you are happy with and talk to them about it. You will need to give them advice on contraception and what is available. You will have to talk through what you think is acceptable. A one-night stand? Sex with the person you love? Sex with someone you are going to live with? You need to think these issues through and communicate with your children. It is vital we do this. We can't leave our children to the whims of our society. In our modern age we need to give our young people all the information they need.

C. THE TALK

Most parents believe that at a given age and on a given day you have to sit down with your son or daughter and have a frank, open talk about the facts of life. The thought of this can cause most parents to have sleepless nights wondering how they can begin the conversation and what they can possibly say. Once that talk is over the subject need never be mentioned again. It's as if the half-hour or so with your child has solved all the problems. A stiff whisky and all is back to normal!

Sadly, that is how a large percentage of parents believe that sex education works. Unfortunately, it is not that simple. Sex education begins almost from the minute that your child is born. It begins with your view of your own sexuality because your child will observe this. They will sense and then observe your attitude towards sex. If, as partners, you do not hold hands or show demonstrable signs of affection, a clear message is given to your children. If you are embarrassed at home about nakedness it communicates a negative message about the body. Sex education must begin by first demonstrating, then teaching, the power of loving relationships. Through our words and actions, we must familiarize our children with the vocabulary of relationships: love, honesty, intimacy, forgiveness and grace.

You need to be giving out healthy, positive images. Do not be embarrassed by the human body, but rather demonstrate a healthy attitude towards it. When they are young let them see you in the bath! This means at a young age they will notice the biological differences and begin to ask questions. Don't avoid them! Don't tell them to go and ask Mummy or Daddy! Obviously their minds will not grasp the major details but they will have positive messages about it. Be demonstrative in front of them. Hold hands when you go for a walk. Kiss each other as you go to work. Again, show that there is nothing to be embarrassed about. A major part of the battle in this area is one of attitude.

As they grow older the questions will get more detailed, but don't avoid them. Tackle them by giving the information that will help your children. This way you are giving them the information little by little. This may mean that there will never be that one big talk that we mentioned earlier, but even if there is the foundation has been laid by you. This is why it's important that from the day of birth a healthy attitude towards the body and sex has been developed. This means that when you begin to talk it will be a natural extension of all that's gone before.

For girls, there is the big question of periods. This can be a very disturbing time. There are many false things said in the schoolyard which lead to some girls developing a wrong understanding of the subject. That is why it is essential that you have talked that matter through with them before it begins to happen. Don't wait for the periods to start and then tell them. Having said all that, you need to be aware that just because you have explained what is going to happen it doesn't mean that you then can forget about it. For many girls, even though they know what is going to happen, it is still a traumatic event. You just need to be there to give help and support.

As your children develop into teenagers the questions and issues become more difficult. You need to have thought through your answers. It may be that you will share your past failures in this area as a way of helping your children. Only you can make the decision about the wisdom of that. But in a world that treats sexual inter-course as a socially accepted part of a night out, you need to have prepared your children to stand against that. They need to realize the value and intimacy of sex and that its greatest value lies in sharing it with only one person.

For your children's sake, tell them everything they need to know, because if you don't somebody else will and we have no control over that. For your children's sake tell them.

1 Don't panic. You may feel desperate, but hang on in there – there is hope and above all your daughter needs you right now.

2 Go on loving her. Whatever you may feel about the situation your daughter needs your unconditional love, so give it to her. The questions can come later.

3 Get yourself some support. Talk about the situation with a trusted friend, and share your feelings. You will need it.

4 Involve the father in any discussions. Whatever you may feel about him, he is the father of your daughter's child and his views are essential. Don't isolate him.

5 If your daughter is still at school talk to her teachers. Consult with your doctor. Get all the advice and support you can for your daughter.

6 There is the issue of abortion. This is a big issue which you need to consider very carefully. To have an abortion will have major implications for your daughter. Ask the advice of your doctor and wise, trusted friends. Do not come to a decision in the heat of the moment but take your time and think it through. My advice is always to have the child.

7 Whatever happens, go on loving your daughter.

ACTION POINTS

◆ In front of the children try to hold hands more often, show more respect for one another, and break down traditional sexual stereotype models.

◆ Find out the sex education policy followed by your children's school. Make sure you are happy with what they are teaching your children. If you are, encourage them, if not, challenge them.

◆ Give your children all the information you can – they need it!

◆ Your children will never be as shocked as you imagine.

◆ At the appropriate time, share your past failures.

The ten most important steps to help your children

1 Value them as unique and special people. Don't stop telling them how proud you are of them.

2 Spend time with them doing what they want to do.

3 Tell them you love them, but do more – demonstrate it by your actions.

4 Always build them up in front of their friends.

5 Ask their advice and *listen* to it,

6 Give them a hug as often as possible.

7 Build bridges for your children to walk over.

8 Remember, you are never too old to say, 'I'm sorry'.

9 Trust your children.

10 Love them through it all.

An end that is really a beginning

Well, we've almost made it to the end. As I finished this book my wife and I went to spend Christmas with my parents. While we were there I learned a simple truth. I've been married for 14 years and have not lived with my parents for 20 years. Yet as we all got set to go for a walk my mother turned to me and asked, 'Now, son, have you got a scarf and hat so that you don't get a cold?'

I was about to answer back and tell her I was old enough to make my own mind up, when I caught myself, smiled and realized the simple truth that my mother and father will *always* be my mother and father. They can't be anything else. You never stop being a parent.

The purpose of this book has been to try to help some of you on that journey of parenthood. It's a hard role, but I believe that if we share our successes and failures then we can help one another. We've looked at some difficult and hard issues – many do not have easy answers. But I hope that we have learned that there *are* ways forward.

The reason this chapter is called *an end that is really a beginning* is for the very reason that we never stop learning. Just because you've read this book or ten others does not mean you've mastered the art of being a parent. Rather, each day will bring its new challenges and a new beginning. But for the sake of our children we need to give it our best shot.

In this book I have tried to help you enter into some of the pressures your children face. I also hope that it has given you some clues as to how you can stand with them through it all.

Whatever you have learned there is one theme that runs throughout the book. The bottom line with all our children – indeed, with all of us – is to know that we are loved. The greatest gift you can give to your child is unconditional love. As a friend of mine has written in a song:

We don't know nothing, we don't know much,
Just an aching and a longing to be loved.[19]

Notes

1 Quoted by Mark Ashton, *Christian Youth Work* (Kingsway, 1986), p.15.

2 David Partington, *Pills, Poppers and Caffeine* (Hodder & Stoughton), p.19.

3 Douglas Coupland, *Shampoo Planet* (Simon & Schuster, 1993).

4 Douglas Coupland, *Life after God* (Simon & Schuster, 1994).

5 Royal College of Psychiatrists, Eating Disorders – Council Report CR14, 1992.

6 US National Centre for Overcoming Overeating, 1996 International No-Diet Day.

7 Carol A. Johnson, *Self-Esteem Comes in All Sizes* (Doubleday Books, 1995).

8 Fiona Malcolm, *Independent*, 17 July 1996.

9 Anita Roddick, *Full Voice: The Body and Self-esteem*, Issue 1 (The Body Shop, 1996).

10 *Q* Magazine, December 1997, p.50.

11 Bryan Appleyard, *Sunday Times Magazine*, 21 December 1997.

12 Richard and Helen Exley (eds.), *To Dad* (Exley Press, 1997), p.1.

13 James Ferman, British Board of Film Classifier, *Panorama*, 27 February 1995.

14 Quoted by Paul Francis, *The Seduction* (HarperCollins, 1995), p.86.

15 Philip Yancey, *What's So Amazing About Grace*? (Zondervan, 1997), pp.49–51. © 1997 Philip D. Yancey. Used by permission of Zondervan Publishing House.

16 Melanie McFadyean, *Drug Wise* (Icon Books, 1997), p.10.

17 Josh McDowell, *Teens Speak Out: 'What I Wish My Parents Knew About My Sexuality'* (Here's Life Publishers, 1987), pp.29–30.

18 Trust for the Study of Adolescence.

19 Martyn Joseph, *An Aching and a Longing* (Alliance Music, 1989).

Also available from Marshall Pickering

You Want To Pierce What?

GETTING A GRIP ON TODAY'S FAMILY

Walker Moore

'This book is not an owner's manual or an instruction book. It is a book that will help you get a firm grip on what your children are facing in the world, and how you can help prepare them for it.' *Dr Walker Moore*

In *You Want To Pierce What?* Dr Moore explores creative ways to bring teenagers into the privileges and responsibilities of adulthood through a covenant with God and their parents. Covering crucial issues such as communication, sexuality, commitment, drugs and alcohol, violence and peer pressure, this book presents challenges to both parents and teenagers.

Complete Prayers for Young People

William Barclay

The bestselling *Prayers for Young People* and *Complete Prayers for Young People* are great introductions to prayer for young Christians. This new omnibus edition brings both books together in one volume for a new generation of readers. It is an ideal gift for anyone who wants to come closer to God but needs guidance to get started.

Prayers for Young People consists of simple morning and evening prayers for each week of the year, to get you thinking and talking to God. *More Prayers for Young People* goes into greater depth with a six-week cycle of Bible passages and prayers from well-known sources. It also includes prayers for difficult situations and special occasions.

'... attractively and invitingly readable ... this is a grand little book.' *Methodist Recorder*

'...g ives practical guidance in a natural and attractive way ...' *Church of England Newspaper*

Pastoral Care for Young People

Edited by Mark Vernon

Perhaps never before have young people faced so many external and internal pressures coming from different directions – the influence of their peers and contemporary culture, the high ratio of broken or dysfunctional families and profound questions about their identity in an uncertain and ever-changing world. Those in youth ministry must expect to find themselves at the cutting edge of the social and emotional crises which teenagers undergo.

This practical handbook aims to provide youth leaders with an in-depth understanding of the pastoral issues they are likely to encounter, together with comprehensive guidelines on appropriate care and counsel. Compiled by Mark Vernon of Oasis Trust, this is an essential resource for youth workers, church leaders and all those with a pastoral concern for the particular needs of young people.

Complete Prayers for Teenagers

Nick Aiken

'Lord, so often I mess up and do what you don't want me to do. It's a huge comfort to know that you forgive me and love me, even when I may not be able to forgive myself. Amen.'

This is just one of the heartfelt, often funny or charming but always honest prayers which Nick Aiken collected from young people all over Britain for *Prayers for Teenagers* and *More Prayers for Teenagers*. Now published as one edition, the prayers are as fresh and as direct as ever.